Once I Forget
Poems

John P. Portelli

*Translated from the Maltese
by Aaron Aquilina and John Martin*

To feel one's attachment to a certain region ... to know that there is always a spot where one's heart will feel at peace — these are many certainties for a single human life. And yet this is not enough. But at certain moments everything yearns for that spiritual home.

       Albert Camus, *Summer in Algiers*

Published by
Daraja Press
https://darajapress.com
Wakefield, Quebec, Canada

© 2025 John P. Portelli

Book design: Kate McDonnell
Cover artwork: Carmel Micallef

ISBN 978-1-997742-16-6

Cataloguing in Publication data is available from
the Library and Archives of Canada

CONTENTS

Preface	vii
Once a Village	1
Forgetting Everything	23
Notes on Author, Translators and Cover Artist	64
Acknowledgments	68

Preface

Time and again, throughout our lives, we turn to poetry and to the open expanses it affords us — in the hope that it may give voice to our own sense of forgetfulness, of loss, of longing, of the wounds and wonders we carry within us. Maybe we do so because we expect poetry to return our own finitude to us in a somewhat altered form. But for how long – for how many times – may such a lease of hope hold out?

As its title suggests, *Once I Forget* puts us on the threshold of what may just be about to occur. Once uttered, that once will provoke a resounding echo and bring about whatever will ensue. In this sense, Portelli's poems refuse to settle for any facile embrace of forgetfulness. On the contrary, they call to mind Pablo Neruda's lasting insight: that forgetting, when even possible at all, is a lengthy and meandering affair. That once-I-forget becomes the poet's own, invaluable gift: a call to shape the outer limits of memory into process, and into poem.

Here, John P. Portelli treads along those nebulous cliff-edges where forgetfulness attempts to pick at the treacherous scabs of recall, capturing the vertigo of a distant childhood as it inches outward into the land's end of metaphor. His poetry gazes into the chasm where the wraiths of a past half-lived and half-written course sensuously through the vanishing present – till they collide, that is, with the reflection of an old man in the mirror.

Roving effortlessly between W.B. Yeats, Gabriela Mistral and Derek Walcott, Portelli pauses along the way for a scotch-and-smoke with Francis Ebejer, literary doyen of Malta's Ħad-Dingli where the poet himself spent his entire youth and part of his childhood.

From its textured earlier poems to its latter, more hermetic pieces, I have sensed in this book the rise of Portelli's epilogic key: the awakening to an encroaching erosion of memory which, here, becomes a more inviting and evocative refuge than the tenacity itself of hope. The flow in Aaron Aquilina's and John Martin's English translation catches Portelli's poetry at its most tactile, as it flirts with the precipice of its own, eminent untranslatability — there, where village keels over vertiginously into verse.

— Prof. Norbert Bugeja, University of Malta

Once a Village

1.

cold was the night
that first night we arrived
that night of exile from the village of my birth
where I played in the streets
in courtyards full of farfugia,
ortensia, snake plant;
it was the night of wreaths
without candle or purification
it was the night which created endless sorrow
it is the night which reminds me always of the loss
of a life I will never forget
it was the night of loneliness,
the cliff's echo my only confessor:
how long do you look for tombs on
faraway seas? astonishment leaves you in awe

2.

you asked who I am
I told you: certainly not one of those
with whom you rub shoulders
for the empty praise of your writings
scrawled on a wall sobbing syllables
it cannot utter because it is too weary
for your passions;
now you melt like the soap
you bought from a tunisian market
scattering the smell of fresh jasmine

what right have you to ask who I am?

and you asked again who I am
i told you: I am an accident
born without willing it
my mother and father could have been other people
my people could have been a different people
my land could have been a land swallowed by the seas

what right have you to ask who I am?
do you know who you are?

but you asked again who I am
I told you: I am one who was born somewhere
where bombs were once dropped
raised in a village crucified by cliffs
howling for the thorns that sprout between the stones
on which once sat the fishermen
who disappeared in the sea

what right have you to ask who I am?
who are you?
and who am I to tell you all this?

3.

the clothes scorched on the summery rooftop
the tomatoes sundried and the seeds ready;
hope is harder than losing it;
I have to rest my head on the branch of an oak tree
continue to wait for the fresh water
of the village pump to spurt anew

4.

hard is the sweetness of departure;
early this morning
the sweet memory of the grapevine I pruned
    forty-four years ago awoke me;
I abandoned it in that red field in a *Ħad-Dingli* vacated
by the memories I took with me,
and today I have almost forgotten where I have hidden
    these bittersweet memories
that pampered me on their lap, far away from the
    sweetness of the vine
today, piteously,
dead
thrown onto the cliffs
with no warning

5.

my childhood balcony hangs ready in the village
that raised and hindered me
waiting for everything to be forgotten here and now

the geraniums on the balcony do not tell the truth
stirring shadows between their leaves
waiting for a different story

the bees uselessly try to provoke sweetness
life is full of surprises
waiting for the end of contingent accidents

6.

let me try to fall in love with the memory
of the village that raised me
embracing the cattle's water pump
embracing the hill leading to church
embracing the doctor's auberge
embracing *Babbas*'s shop
embracing *The Swallows*' Football Club
embracing the alleyways
embracing the windmills
embracing *Red Paul*'s farmhouse
embracing the song of barn swallows
scared of the cliff's boulders
that once almost ended me;
allow me to try
embracing
better than hanging myself

7.

tough is that village hill, and the ropes
abandoned on pavements tied
to the past, and the knots too tight,
the hawkers' shouts deafeningly silent,
the gardens today have neither peaches nor nectarines;
now the shadows of the alleys play only
with the discordant peals of old bells
not wishing for any life, neither yesterday's
nor today's nor tomorrow's — nothing
has purpose, the movement of memory lost:
the ghosts will soon come to dance in the square

8.

today the village that raised me is sleeping
in the hidden drawers of my aging mind,
far away from it, among the oak trees
and the maples which always tell all,
except the sweetness of the breeze and my village ordeals,
and the swallows' song always lost
as the tired self looks but never finds,
picking at the scabs of a sorrowful past,
comforted now by loves bygone
memories of my parents' tombs
forever at rest in the village that awaits me

9.

nothing remains as it is
my soul grows cold waiting for the beginning
it rebels against the face of power
and attempting to love you was useless
your cliffs are too steep
terrifying the swallows

uselessly you waited for me
uselessly you hoped
I left
and you
how long will you wait in vain?

I know I have been proud
cast you aside
today on your hills
even the sharp rocks of the garigue
the thorns and parched thyme pull me towards them

the deep vicious sea enchants me
the acrobatic swallows comfort me

fulfilment is in nothing
and I am here
forever afraid that I will not see you again
because I created my own exile
without place
everyday
without time

10.

I have filled in my notebook on both sides
as stuffed as a courgette ready for baking
in the village oven
where everyone lets slip their truth
imqarrun chicken potatoes baked rice
pork with onions and fennel
and in their midst
the hidden wishes that flew from the notebook
seeking rest
dripping ink

11.

no one jokes around with death
in front of whom we praise even enemies
and Ċensu the village warden
was always dreaming
of leaving for the city
partying, dancing with the most beautiful girls
but never cultivated the will
to cross frontiers
and this morning left us
a great leap
and everyone saluted our Ċensu,
who embraced his desires
only in his dreams

12.

you would sit every day behind the *antiporta*
looking through almost transparent curtains;
who knows what you say, or what you hear?
maybe you were watching for *Karmenu*, the kerosene seller,
or the idiotic greengrocer or the feeble baker
or the merchant who would come once a week
from the south selling bloomers of all colours;
you were the village news
you knew all the new lovers
reading their hearts from their eyes;
no birth, no death escaped you
and the footballers would stop to talk to you after each game
there behind the *antiporta* often in religious silence;
and how happy you were when your younger brother
arrived from the field with cabbage, potato, and cauliflower
and happier when your grandchildren paid their weekly visit
wreathing their hair with flowers;
there behind the *antiporta* you would dream of the
    cliffs of your childhood
waiting for you daily, not yet losing heart
because your heart still beats with the hope
planted by your mother and father in red fields
with hay that never tires of greeting the sky
which in my day was afraid of the sea's ferocity,
today calm, stroked by the swallows' songs;
I do not know when this sea will evaporate
now that the sun has lost its mind blazing with full strength
and who knows what happened to that *antiporta* and curtains?!

13.

I was tempted by you
I smoked a cigar
drank a double whisky neat
forgot *Ħad-Dingli*
the exaggerated humility of homeland;
I was consoled by memories of
Menz, Vaganzi tas-Sajf,
L-Imnarja Żmien il-Qtil,
and *In the Eye of the Sun*
and with the drops of blood
there started another tragedy;
useless for it to cover itself with a long red scarf
and the smoke of the cigar
distracts the spirit's dizziness,
impatient

14.

this morning I visited the village of my youth
searching for steps that have forever disappeared
from the streets and alleys and squares
and did not hear the playing children's voices
or the peals of discordant bells
or the merchants' shouts beside the church
or the whining of cats and abandoned dogs.
I tethered myself to a bench in the main square
until at sundown I spied souls
ceaselessly wailing the end of time
and the saddening statue of the dramaturge.
it is difficult to drag the nets of your youth
before you had left for that endless exile

15.

and even when memory fails me
as some wizened tree in the village square
where we played with no sense of time, unknowingly
borrowed everyone's happiness,
and teased whoever came our way, hoping to escape the gloom
awaiting the heavy strikes of noon, melting
in the sun's fury as a jellyfish stranded on the shore
pulling it towards the crazed cliffs of life's home
expecting to escape the lost swallows
desiring the west hidden in the future's fog...

16.

today I visited the cliffs
of the village that raised me
glowing with summery sadness
weighed down with western waves
always there, blank,
today parching the thyme
crying over windborne swallows
and the painted *madliena* besieged
vigilant and calmly measured

and he recognised me and commanded:
"take me with you, take me with you."

how can I ever forget you?
you are my rock and my shelter
I am the metaphor.

17.

I greeted you and sent you my eyes
to see you properly
I gave you even my nostrils
to smell your proper scent
I slid my heart towards you
a shoulder for your virtues
I loved you with your faults
I loved you with your beauty
I craved you in stillness
and now you have disappeared without a sound
without the groaning of your desires
I am lost

every day I wait
for your consoling shadow
an augur of your attractions:
how have you escaped?

and now the memories only in mirrors
your time is also lost
and in the village's secluded square
the old man snoozes in the sun
waiting
uselessly
for death

18.

this morning even the angels descended
onto the cliffs of your childhoods
joyfully flitting with the memories
of kisses on benches
almost opposite *Filfla*
where you hugged in secrecy
smoked a cigarette or two
to numb the sensations sadness
of your love
each day walking the edge
thinking of jumping
into that profound azure
somewhat existential
inviting
inviting

19.

very early this morning
the memory of the vine's sweetness awoke me;
I pruned it forty-four years ago,
I abandoned it, withered
in that red field
in a *Ħad-Dingli* vacated
by the memories I took with me,
and today I have almost forgotten where I have hidden
these bittersweet memories
that pampered me on their lap,
far away from the sweetness of the vine
today, piteously,
dead
thrown onto the cliffs
with no warning

20.

burn for me the olive leaves
as a cleansing by incense
from all the virtuous vices
burn for me, burn
so sweet is the white smoke
gather the salt in your fist
circle, circle above your head
and throw it behind your back
throw it in water
and purify yourself
and smoke, smoke once more;
in the middle of the village square
a solitary cedar
and under its shadow
a mummified cat

21.

when the sun might reappear
my hair, falling out,
will float forever on the winds
swaying with the holy rhythms of orthodox chants
dreaming and settling wherever there is shelter to be found:
Agios o Theos
whatever is gone no one can bring back
they used to say in the village
I wrestle, bounded by this existence;
how could it have been otherwise?

Forgetting Everything

1.

let me forget it all, the heart's
hard task, to resist death from the start —
but the day's footsteps never turn back,
from your lips drips the last drop of drink
that has confused you; you wait for what
doesn't exist, not for you nor the others

Once I Forget

2.

and now that this frail body has almost decayed
we may speak of how and why we have met;
now that gales have erased every memory
we may warble what maybe we recall
and so begin:
the bays utterly barren
the sea murmuring in vain

3.

today I met the young man I wanted once
to have been; we walked together in lost woods
sheltering from the shadows
between us a great chasm;
we did our best to embrace but
time was moving too fast

4.

the tree of the past has withered
and we felled it,
scattered the leaves and branches over the cliff
where there seeps the spring of
never-vanishing wishes
and our calm steps always on the water's
surface

5.

the caravan of dust never stops
drifting, dispersing over once-forgotten cities
today endowed with many desires;
perhaps one day we'll find the tombs of the future

6.

today all creation is witness to exile:
the sea of blood ripples
the fields yearn for slumbering clover
the living memorials of the dead
and the needles of memory pierce;
one day we might learn to accept
life

7.

too heavy is the pebble of your life
which you gave me long ago,
smooth and grey,
I now glimpse your face on its back
smiling at me as it once did—
in vain I try to kiss it

8.

we share the same life, the sea and I:
recline against the jagged sharp cliffs
hiding in the caverns;
share the same vices, the sea and I:
stare at the west in endless amazement
consoled by the cry of the lost swallow;
share the same ending, the sea and I:
a letter forgotten in a letterbox

9.

I hug you until the sea shivers
and the waves carve my name
on the necklace I gave you long ago
forever releasing the smell of purple lavender
that I gathered in my youth from heart's collapse

Once I Forget

10.

I always sing to this life
my name in her, her name in me
and now I hug her
her red lips imprinted on my face
I forget every era

11.

your smile drips onto blotting paper
creating new lifeforms
boasting of their lives
starving for the sensation of you

12.

featureless and silenced is this untrembling night
and any time we meet again
wherever we meet
whenever we meet
however we meet
bring me joy with the silence of your body
without boundaries
and your eyes become home
forever

13.

here near this evergreen willow
I long for your love
while life wearies of seeking meaning
and the willow weeps once more
ceaselessly

14.

this morning you wrote to remind me
how your face reminded me
of the juice of Andalusian oranges
and this old body struggles to kill itself
so that it sprouts new life
this time maybe
full of love

15.

and tonight you wrote to remind me
that my place is neither here nor there
between Mars and Jupiter;
let the planets discard all news of us
even now that our bodies have withered
and as we were warned by the wise:
love is all fiction

16.

as in my youth you hugged me
and I became sparkling water spurting from the spring
in tree-shadows budding always without cease—
unlike me;
thank goodness for the illusion of love
that is likely one day to bud from fields buried
in the past

17.

the old man who appeared in the mirror reminded me
love perhaps comes from nothing
where nothing makes sense
not even love
singing the sadness of loss
at the precipice of happy tears

18.

I will not sing any more
except the song of the sadness of loss
before it has happened,
let the language of pure air guide me
to where I never dared wander
and shut my eyes so all space
is engulfed

19.

and now the night is quiet
although all flowers have faded
their perfume inhaled by lungs
fighting for breath in an unknown body
and you turn over a page in the book
you have been reading since birth

20.

when will you utter a word?
without your words life's rhythm weakens;
in vain I look at the mirror
hoping some life will sprout
all news of love discarded

21.

what is it worth that love purifies?
my body does not connect with
the dreams lost in the speech of dead pages
creating only delusion,
once more I walk serene in the woods
scented with flowers and spices
and remain there even through the night
trembling in front of the flickering candle

22.

you and I are as jellyfish
which the sea plays with
until it engulfs us or spews us
onto the shore, sunbathing death,
everything happens as if it were nothing:
not even a whimper
not even a memory

23.

and now I go back to this weak body
that knows nothing, believes nothing
railing against deceitful love
as grey sky toys with grey sky
waiting for lightning to burn bygone letters
whose smell will purify once more those dusty books

24.

in your eyes I glimpse my own reflected;
I realised your eyes are nothing but mine
which see only what they want to see
now they have wearied of looking

25.

I have no hope, not in life
not in death
and perhaps this is for the best:
I surrender, forgetting everything

26.

and that is how our dreams
lose themselves in the mute fountain's flow
alive only in singular loneliness
kept at the surface of clouded water
stagnant

27.

this morning I washed my hands
in running water
awaiting the play of the moment,
and you are gone again in the features of childhood
and the trees of every love let go their leaves

28.

sunset strangles all the words
you used to say as you held
yourself in the open spaces buried today
under dry desires—
where you wait for even a single drop

29.

your eyes glare from the living tomb
which is starved of your desire lost among the souls
who search for respite in the action of the past,
and you scratch at the lid of the suspicious present;
the schism between your blood and his
casts doubt

30.

we never shared our secrets
they remained hidden
like the underside of a leaf
perhaps mildewed
perhaps pristine,
and the sensations of love
creep along the stems
without any sense of order

31.

the silent snow that fell throughout the night
as white carnations without scent
as a formless map:
in vain it looks for the path
hoping that the cold will never stop
guarding the frontiers of loss

32.

and now the rain is torrential
over the hills which look for your love;
you have left to wander some other land
in your mind the promise
of never forgetting the old ways
of our childhood

33.

your drops of love have become pouring rain
the emptiness within you deafened
but filled only with pangs of sorrow;
perhaps one day this rain will turn to snow
and ease the weight of solidity

Once I Forget

34.

since the rain has become snow
we have lit sage to sanctify our bodies,
bit by bit our chests filled with holy smoke
and our minds and hearts met for just a moment:
spontaneous lovers without thought
ready to fend off every chill
horning their fingers to ward off the evil eye

35.

tonight the hawk pecks away at life on a snowy roof
never finishing
and hides all evidence
hoping that it will one day be set free
—as have you—
before spring arrives

36.

you said this morning you did not want the fate of Sisyphus;
you smashed the boulder of frozen snow
eagerly you shattered it
gathered the pieces without beginning or end
and left, your footsteps crunching

37.

the story could almost be over now:
everything inevitable has happened
nothing new remains
even the dripping from the ruined well
has stopped
the exiled have all fled—
except for you

38.

your heart a bouquet of abandonment's red roses
losing a petal a day
fearing to tread on the dark earth
lest you crack it
and sweetness rises to greet the planets' apathy;
maybe some day they might smile at you
and you could once again embrace

39.

today the workers of existence
have slept a long and fitful sleep
and from the silence of this destiny
words have caught fire
and the ashes are scattered
between fulfilment and its absence

40.

afraid of the edge between fulfilment and its absence
poetry nonetheless continues to regenerate
resisting between freedom and restrictions
shedding desires with no sign of weakness
and I wait
one day I will meet it
more or less as I once met you

Notes on Author, Translators and Cover Artist

John P. Portelli, originally from Malta, is a professor emeritus in the Department of Social Justice Education at the University of Toronto. He has taught in Canadian universities since 1982. Besides eleven academic books, he has published eleven collections of poetry, two collections of short stories (one translated into English and published as *Everyday Encounters*), and a novel, *Everyone but Faiza* (Burlington, ON: Word and Deed, 2021).

His literary work has been translated into Italian, Romanian, Greek, Farsi, Turkish, Serbian, Urdu, Arabic, Korean, English, Spanish, Portuguese, and Polish. His collection *Here Was* was translated and published in Romanian in June 2023, in Arabic in November 2023, in Italian in January 2024, in Farsi in February 2024, in Turkish in May 2024. *Here Was* was short-listed for the Canadian Book Club Award in October 2024.

Five of his books have been short-listed for the Malta Book Council Annual Literary Award. His latest two collections of poetry are *The Shadow: Poems for Gaza* (October 2024), co-authored with Ahmed Miqdad, and *Unsilenced: Poems for Gaza* (Malta: Horizons, and Quebec, Canada: Daraja Press, April 2025). He now lives between Toronto and Malta and beyond.

Aaron Aquilina is an academic with the University of Malta's Department of English. His academic work navigates literature, theory, and philosophy, and comprises various articles, book chapters, an edited collection, and a monograph (*The Ontology of Death*, Bloomsbury, 2023). He has also published poetry in journals such as *Orbis, Stand, The International Human Rights Arts Journal*, and several others. He is the founding and current editor-in-chief of the University of Malta's international creative writing journal, *ANTAE* (www.um.edu.mt/antae).

John Martin is a retired barrister whose working life was mainly spent in law and community centres dealing with housing, welfare, and immigration problems. He studied Languages at Cambridge and has published 14 volumes of poetry. He has also written plays, some of which have been performed on community radio and at amateur dramatic society readings.

Carmel Micallef was educated at St. Aloysius College and followed a five year course at the Malta School of Art. In 1976 he won first and third prizes in the Malta Amateur Art Competition and Exhibition. Micallef participated in many collective exhibitions in Malta, England, Germany, Greece, USA and Australia, and has held nine personal exhibitions: two at the Fine Arts Museum in Valletta and one in Germany. He won first prize in the Reader's Exhibited Works Competition organized by 'The Artists' magazine of the UK.

Portelli's gorgeous poems speak of exile, searching, and loss in such a way that the reader becomes one with the village of his birth, the cliffs, the smells, his frail body, and the sea.

— Jennifer Hosein

Even in translation, the poetry of Portelli comes to us wrapped in the caul of his Maltese mother tongue. "Guided by the language of pure air," the poems of *Once I Forget* restore our faith in the transcendence of the lyric, in the power of song and secular psalm. These are poems borne of the sorrow of exile and a nostalgia balanced by the knowledge that it is impossible to return: a longing not just for the Malta of the poet's youth, but for "the young man I wanted once to have been," and for the love "who asked who I am."

— Karen Shenfeld

Acknowledgments

Special thanks to Aaron Aquilina and John Martin for the careful translations.

I also thank Professor Norbert Bugeja for the preface, Jennifer Hosein and Karen Shenfeld for the endorsements, and Carmel Micallef for the artwork of the cover.

Thanks to Daraja Press and Horizons for publishing this collection, and for their continued support.

MANY THANKS
JOHN

EU Safety Information

Publisher: Daraja Press, PO BOX 99900 BM 735 664 Wakefield, QC J0X 0C2, Canada
info@darajapress.com | https://darajapress.com

EU Authorized GPSR Representative: Easy Access System Europe – Mustamäe tee 50, 10621 Tallinn, Estonia, gpsr.requests@easproject.com

For EU product safety concerns, please contact us at info@darajapress.com

www.ingramcontent.com/pod-product-compliance
Lightning Source LLC
Chambersburg PA
CBHW060502110426
42738CB00055B/2595